My Neighborhood
The Grocery Store

Megan Cuthbert

LET'S READ
AV2
BY WEIGL
ADDED VALUE • AUDIO VISUAL

www.av2books.com

LET'S READ AV2 BY WEIGL™
ADDED VALUE • AUDIO VISUAL

Go to **www.av2books.com**, and enter this book's unique code.

BOOK CODE

J319716

AV² **by Weigl** brings you media enhanced books that support active learning.

AV² provides enriched content that supplements and complements this book. Weigl's AV² books strive to create inspired learning and engage young minds in a total learning experience.

Your AV² Media Enhanced books come alive with...

Audio
Listen to sections of the book read aloud.

Video
Watch informative video clips.

Embedded Weblinks
Gain additional information for research.

Try This!
Complete activities and hands-on experiments.

Key Words
Study vocabulary, and complete a matching word activity.

Quizzes
Test your knowledge.

Slide Show
View images and captions, and prepare a presentation.

... and much, much more!

Published by AV² by Weigl
350 5th Avenue, 59th Floor New York, NY 10118
Websites: www.av2books.com   www.weigl.com

Library of Congress Control Number: 2014940865

ISBN 978-1-4896-1322-6 (hardcover)
ISBN 978-1-4896-1323-3 (softcover)
ISBN 978-1-4896-1324-0 (single user eBook)
ISBN 978-1-4896-1325-7 (multi-user eBook)

Printed in the United States of America in North Mankato, Minnesota
1 2 3 4 5 6 7 8 9 0 18 17 16 15 14

052014
WEP150314

Project Coordinators: Heather Kissock and Katherine Balcom
Design: Mandy Christiansen

Every reasonable effort has been made to trace ownership and to obtain permission to reprint copyright material. The publishers would be pleased to have any errors or omissions brought to their attention so that they may be corrected in subsequent printings.

Weigl acknowledges Getty Images as the primary image supplier for this title.

The Grocery Store

CONTENTS

This is my neighborhood.

The grocery store is in my neighborhood.

A grocery store is a place where my family goes to buy food.

Eggs
Butter
Bread
Soap
Sugar

We make a list of what food we need to buy.

The grocery store has many aisles filled with shelves.

Most grocery stores carry more than 40,000 things for sale.

Food is sorted by groups in each aisle.

We can find apples with the other kinds of fruit.

11

Labels tell us what is inside a can.

Reading a label can help us make a healthy choice.

Some labels have a date on them.

14

The date tells us how long a food is safe to eat.

The price of each food is printed on the shelf.

16

We read the price so that we know how much each food costs.

Sometimes the grocery store is very busy.

18

I push the cart carefully so that no one gets hurt.

The cashier tells us how much money we need to pay.

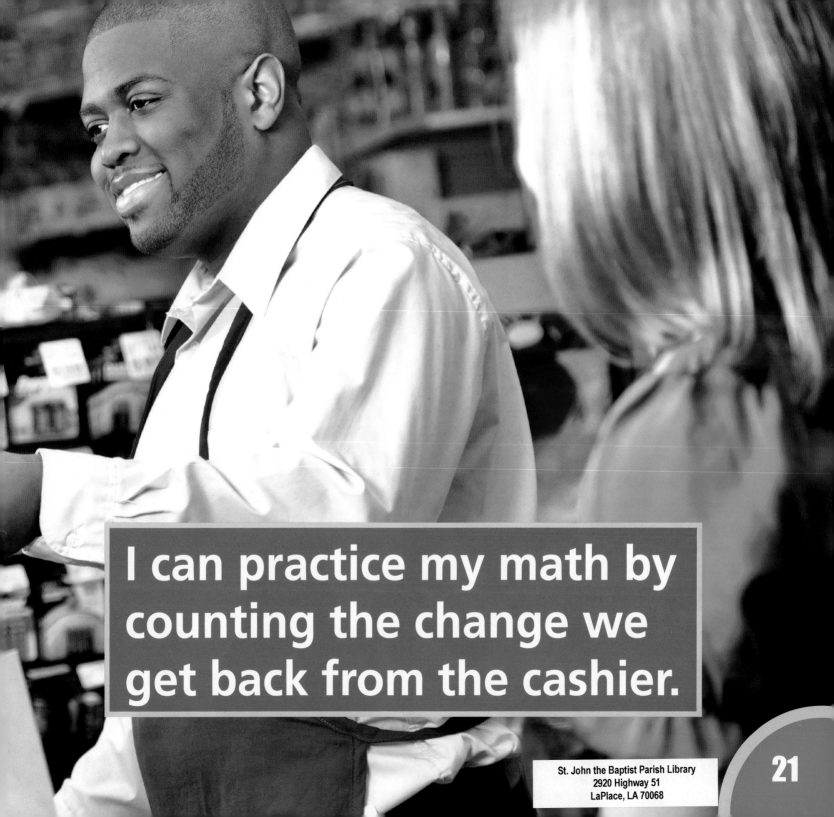

I can practice my math by counting the change we get back from the cashier.

See what you have learned about grocery stores.

Which of these pictures does not show a grocery store?

23

KEY WORDS

Research has shown that as much as 65 percent of all written material published in English is made up of 300 words. These 300 words cannot be taught using pictures or learned by sounding them out. They must be recognized by sight. This book contains 56 common sight words to help young readers improve their reading fluency and comprehension. This book also teaches young readers several important content words, such as proper nouns. These words are paired with pictures to aid in learning and improve understanding.

Page	Sight Words First Appearance
4	is, my, this
5	in, the
6	family, food, place, to, where
7	a, make, need, of, what, we
8	has, many, with
9	carry, for, more, most, than, things
10	by, each, groups
11	can, find, kinds, other
12	tell, us
13	help
14	have, on, some, them
15	eat, how, long
17	know, much, read, so, that
18	sometimes, very
19	gets, I, no, one
20	back, change, from

Page	Content Words First Appearance
4	neighborhood
5	grocery store
7	list
8	aisles, shelves
11	apples, fruit
12	can, labels
13	choice
14	date
16	price, shelf
13	costs
19	cart
20	cashier, money
21	math

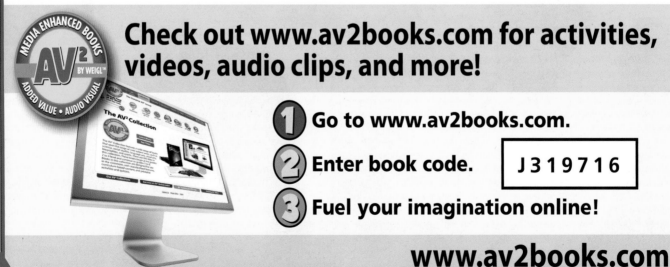

Check out www.av2books.com for activities, videos, audio clips, and more!

1 Go to www.av2books.com.

2 Enter book code. J 3 1 9 7 1 6

3 Fuel your imagination online!

www.av2books.com